SCHOLASTIC QUIZ SCIENCE

Shobhit Mahajan teaches Physics at the University of Delhi. He has written several books on popular science for children. He also writes regularly for newspapers and magazines.

For the Late Shri B.C. Jain, whom I tried, and failed, to convince of the validity of scientifc truth.

Published by Scholastic India Pvt. Ltd.
A subsidiary of Scholastic Inc., New York, 10012 (USA).
Publishers since 1920, with international operations in Canada, Australia, New Zealand, the United Kingdom, India, and Hong Kong.

For information regarding permission, write to:
Scholastic India Pvt. Ltd.
Golf View Corporate Tower-A, 3rd Floor,
DLF Phase V, Gurgaon 122002 (India)

Typeset in Book Antiqua by Mantra Virtual Services, New Delhi

First edition:
Reprinted June November 2019

ISBN-13: 978-81-8477-476-4

Printed at Ram Printograph, Delhi

SCHOLASTIC QUIZ

SCIENCE

Shobhit Mahajan

SCHOLASTIC
New York Toronto London Auckland
Sydney New Delhi Hong Kong

CONTENTS

Questions

Physics 1

Astronomy and Space Science 13

Mathematics 21

Chemistry and Life Sciences 31

Technology 43

Answers

Physics 56

Astronomy and Space Science 64

Mathematics 68

Chemistry and Life Sciences 73

Technology 80

PHYSICS

1. In 2009, the world's most powerful particle accelerator was supposed to start operating, but suffered a technical setback and had to be closed down. What is the name of this accelerator and where is it located?

2. Scientists are hoping to find a new elementary particle with the particle accelerator mentioned above. The existence of this elusive particle, sometimes referred to as the 'God Particle', was predicted more than 40 years ago and is thought to be the key element in understanding the world of elementary particles. What is the name of this particle?

3. According to our current understanding of elementary particles, protons and neutrons are made up of more fundamental particles. What are these called?

4. Quantum chromodynamics (QCD) is the name of the theory of interactions between strongly interacting particles. What does the 'chromo' in this refer to?

5. The work for which Einstein got the Nobel Prize in Physics in 1921 was:

(i) Theory of Special Relativity
(ii) Theory of Brownian Motion
(iii) Photoelectric Effect
(iv) Theory of General Relativity

6. This Italian scientist developed the first nuclear reactor. He also has an element, a class of particles as well as the biggest particle accelerator in the US, named after him. Who is this scientist?

7. The Manhattan Project was:

(i) a project to clean up the sewage system in New York.

(ii) the name given to the reconstruction of the World Trade Centre in New York.

(iii) a project to extract wave energy from tidal waves on the island of Manhattan in New York.

(iv) a top-secret project which developed the first atomic bomb in 1945.

8. This English scientist is most well known for formulating the atomic theory. He was colour blind and developed a theory of colour blindness which was proved to be wrong. However, his name has become a common term for colour blindness. Who was he?

9. The hydrogen atom is made up of a proton and an electron. A very similar system exists with an electron and a positron (the antiparticle of an electron). What is this called?

10. There are __________ number of natural elements and the heaviest natural element is __________.

11. This scientist led the development of the first atomic bomb and had a deep interest in Hindu philosophy. On seeing the first atomic bomb test, he is reported to have quoted from the *Bhagavad Gita*, "Now I have become Death, the Destroyer of worlds". Who was this scientist?

12. This Austrian scientist is known as one of the founders of quantum mechanics. He is also known for his path-breaking book, *What is Life* wherein he proposed that very complex molecules might be the basis of genetics. Who was this scientist?

13. This element was first seen in the spectrum of the Sun and is in fact named after the Greek word for Sun. It is a colourless, odourless gas and is the second most abundant element in the universe. Which element is this?

14. The Helium nucleus has 2 protons and 2 neutrons. If we add 1 neutron to the Helium nucleus, we get:

(i) Hydrogen

(ii) Helium

(iii) Lithium

(iv) Boron

15. Atoms emit light when:

(i) the nucleus absorbs a neutron.

(ii) an elecron falls from a higher to a lower energy state.

(iii) an electron revolves around the nucleus.

(iv) laser light is shone upon them.

16. Why do aluminium cans containing deodorant sprays, soft drinks, etc. have a curved base?

17. This principle was discovered by a famous Swiss-Dutch mathematician in the 18th century and is used in a variety of things from the carburettor in petrol engines to measuring fluid flow rates. Name the mathematician and the principle.

18. If the time period for oscillation of a pendulum of length 4 feet is 2 seconds, what will be the length of a pendulum with a time period of 1 second?

19. In 1696, the famous scientist Isaac Newton became the head of a very important government entity in Britain. This entity was:

i) The British House of Lords

ii) The Royal Mint

iii) Greenwich Observatory

iv) Cambridge University

20. The SI (International Systems of Units) unit of pressure is named after this famous French scientist who made important contributions to the study of fluids. He was also a pioneer in developing the science of probability. Who was this scientist?

21. What is common between a crowbar used to lift a heavy stone, the wheelbarrow used to carry the stone, and the elbow joint in the arm that carries the load?

22. The direction of flow of air in a cyclone depends on whether the cyclone is in the Northern or the Southern hemisphere. This effect, caused by the rotation of the earth, is named after a French mathematician who first studied it. What was the name of the mathematician?

23. A device used for measuring and maintaining orientation of a moving body relies on the law of conservation of angular momentum. This device is indispensible for space travel, satellites, aeroplanes, missiles, etc. What is this device called?

24. Ball bearings in your bicycle wheel (and many other machines) work on a simple principle of physics. What is this principle?

25. Gears are used in a lot of moving devices—from clocks to cars. One of the main functions of the gears is to

provide gear reduction in transmission of power from the motor to the moving part (wheel, hands of a clock, etc). There is another type of gear which is used to change the direction of motion. What are these gears called?

26. The rate of change of ______________ is due to the net external force on a body.

27. The longest total solar eclipse possible is:

(i) about 5 minutes.

(ii) about 20 minutes.

(iii) slightly more than 7 minutes and 30 seconds.

(iv) depends on the season and the year.

28. During a total solar eclipse, sometimes spots of bright light are visible after the first contact of the lunar disc with the solar disc. These are called Bailey's Beads. What is the cause of this phenomenon?

29. A lunar eclipse occurs:

(i) only on full moon nights.

(ii) only on nights with three quarters of the moon.

(iii) at any time.

(iv) only on new moon nights.

30. Viscosity is the measure of resistance that a fluid offers against forces which make it flow. Thus, motor oil is more viscous than water. What is the study of viscosity called?

31. The telescope used by Galileo to observe the moons of Jupiter was a refracting telescope which used refraction of light by lenses to magnify the image. Another kind of telescope, called the reflecting telescope, uses curved mirrors to form an image and was invented by a famous scientist in 1668. Who was the scientist?

32. Glass is made from the same material as sand. True or false?

33. Polaroid cameras (cameras which allow instant photographs) were invented by this American scientist. He also invented inexpensive polarising filters for light which are used in the 3-D glasses needed to see films like *Avatar*. What was the name of this scientist?

34. This kind of microscope, invented in the 1930s by Fritz Zernicke, allows for the viewing of biological samples without staining them with reagents. In particular, this allows one to observe the complete cell cycle. What is the name of the technique?

35. Lasers are now being extensively used in a variety

of areas—from barcode readers to corrective eye surgery and even surveying equipment. Lasers operate usually in the optical part of the spectrum and were invented in 1960. However, the principle on which lasers work was discovered in 1953 with the development of a kind of device which did the same for microwave radiation. What was this device called?

36. When light propagates in a vacuum, the product of the frequency and wavelength of light is a universal constant. What is this constant and what is its value?

37. Where in our body is one likely to find rods, cones and photosensitive ganglion cells?

38. The formation of a rainbow on a rainy day is due to the combination of two optical phenomena. Name the phenomena?

39. Light waves are transverse in nature, like the waves on a string where the disturbance is in a direction perpendicular to the direction of motion of the wave. What is the nature of sound waves?

40. What is the frequency range of sound waves that can be heard by the human ear?

41. The *F-18* aircraft used by the US Air Force has a maximum speed of Mach 1.8. What does the term 'Mach' refer to?

42. In thermodynamics, an isothermal process is one which is carried out by keeping the temperature of a system constant. What is an adiabatic process?

43. Temperature is a measure of ________________ of the particles of any system.

44. The minimum temperature which is achievable by any process whatsoever is called absolute zero. How much is absolute zero on the Celsius scale of temperature?

45. Suppose one could build an ideal internal combustion engine of the kind used in automobiles. This ideal engine would have no heat losses or frictional losses of any kind. Would it be possible to extract 100% of the chemical energy which is stored in the petrol with such an engine?

46. "Heat cannot flow spontaneously by itself from a hotter body to a colder body". This commonsensical statement is actually a very important law of Physics which governs the ultimate fate of the universe. What law is this?

47. The term 'electricity' is derived from the Latin term 'electricus' which itself is derived from the Greek word 'elektron'. What does 'elektron' mean?

48. This famous Italian doctor in the 18th century conducted experiments on the effects of electricity

on frogs and laid the foundations of bioelectricity. A very important electrical instrument is named after him. Who was he?

49. We know that substances like iron, steel, nickel are attracted by a magnetic field. These substances are called paramagnetic substances. There are however some substances which are repelled by a magnetic field. What are these called?

50. The electrical supply that we get from the mains is __________ current while that obtained from a battery is ____________ current.

51. What is piezoelectric effect?

52. A diode is an electrical device which has two electrodes and is used as a kind of valve to allow current in only one direction. How many electrodes does a tetrode have?

53. What is the basic difference between an internal combustion engine and an external combustion engine? Which kind of engine is used in an automobile?

54. When a parachutist jumps from the airplane, after a while he attains a constant velocity due to air resistance. What is this velocity called?

55. Most of you have seen a golf ball. It is a very hard, white ball with a lot of dimples on its surface. What

is the purpose of these dimples?

56. The frequency of the sound waves used in ultrasound of the human body is:

(i) 250 kHz - 2000 kHz

(ii) 20 Hz – 20 kHz

(iii) 2000 KHz - 20000 kHz

(iv) 2 Hz - 20 Hz

57. The density of ice made from freshwater is .917 gm/cc and hence it floats in water which has a density of 1 gm/cc. When an ice cube floats in water, roughly what fraction of its volume is below water?

58. A guitar string is 25 cm long between the two edges. What is the wavelength of the fundamental note that this string produces?

59. At what angle must a shotput be thrown so that it goes the maximum horizontal distance?

60. The electricity used in our houses is at a voltage of 220V. However, the danger signs pasted near transmission lines typically show a much higher voltage (11000V, 22000 V, etc). Why is electric power transmitted at such high voltages rather than at 220V at which it is used?

ASTRONOMY AND SPACE SCIENCE

1. In 1543, as this famous Polish astronomer lay dying, he was given the first printed copy of his revolutionary book, *De Revolutionibus Orbium Coelestium* (*On the Revolutions of the Celestial Spheres*) which had just been printed. Legend has it that the astronomer had one look at the book and died immediately thereafter. Who was this astronomer?

2. In astronomy, what does the acronym AGN refer to?

3. Beyond the planet Neptune in our solar system, there exists a region which is similar to the asteroid belt but is mainly made up of ice. This region is believed to contain hundreds of thousands of mostly small objects, though the total mass of this region is less than 10% of the Earth's mass. What is this region called?

4. Astronomers believe that almost all the comets originate in this spherical region which extends to a distance of almost one light year from the Sun. What is this region called?

5. The speed of our Sun, within the Milky Way galaxy, is ________ km/sec and it takes ____________ years to complete one revolution of the galactic centre.

6. This is the largest satellite in the solar system and in fact is larger than the planet Mercury. Which satellite

is this and around which planet does it orbit?

7. Olympus Mons is the highest known mountain in the solar system. It stands about 27 km in height (about thrice as high as Mount Everest) and is roughly 550 km wide. Where is it located?

8. A solar day on this planet is approximately 176 Earth days long while a solar 'year' lasts about 88 Earth days. The orbit of this planet around the Sun is the most eccentric of all planets. Which planet is this?

9. In 1675, an Italian astronomer Giovanni Cassini discovered a region around a planet. This region appears as a gap between two objects and is now known as the Cassini Division in his honour. Where is it located?

10. This planet is known as the 'Vacuum Cleaner of the Solar System' because it receives the maximum number of impacts from comets. Which planet is this?

11. In 1781, William Herschel discovered the first planet which was not known to the ancients. This planet was also the first to be discovered with the help of a telescope. Which planet is this?

12. In 1931, this engineer was the first to identify a radio source in space using a radio antenna that was

built for studying interference in short wave radio communications. The unit of radio flux is now named in his honour. Who was this engineer?

13. COBE is an acronym for:

(i) the zoological name of a kind of cobra found in Western Congo.

(ii) the satellite which studied the cosmic microwave background radiation.

(iii) a galaxy which is shaped like a cube.

(iv) an award given for gallantry in military service in the United Kingdom.

14. In the spectrum of sunlight, one finds that there are dark bands or groups of finely spaced lines because of absorption of certain wavelengths in the outer part of the Sun. These lines were first discovered by a German optician in the 18th century and provide invaluable information about the composition of the Sun. What are these lines called?

15. This star was used by the ancient Egyptians to base their calendar. The rising of this star on the eastern horizon, just before the summer solstice also happened just before the predictable annual flooding of the Nile. Which star was this?

16. Sirius, the dog star, is the brightest star in the night

sky. It is actually a binary star system and the bright Sirius A star has a companion star, Sirius B, which is much dimmer. What kind of a star is Sirius B?

17. ______________________ was an Indian astronomer who was the head of the astronomical observatory at Ujjain and during his tenure there wrote a text on astronomy, the *Brahmasphutasiddhanta* in 628AD.

18. SN1987A and SN1006 describe massive explosive events in the universe—explosions which in a few seconds produce more energy than an entire galaxy. They were first recorded by Chinese astronomers in 185AD and have recently been in the news since they are being used as accurate cosmic distance ladders. What are these events?

19. In cosmology, it is a known fact that the speed with which a distant galaxy moves away from us, depends on the distance to the galaxy. This law is named after a famous American astronomer who was a pioneer in measuring cosmic distances. NASA has named the space telescope after him. Who was this astronomer?

20. In 1919, the famous astronomer, Arthur Eddington, undertook an expedition to Africa to measure the bending of starlight by the Sun during a total solar eclipse. His results, which were widely reported,

confirmed a theory which is now accepted as the correct theory of gravitation. Which theory was this?

21. The first man-made object to go into space was:

(i) The German *V2* rocket made during World War II

(ii) *Sputnik*

(iii) *Vanguard 1*

(iv) *Apollo 1*

22. When a spacecraft is launched, astronauts feel a tremendous force pushing them on their seats which is said to be 5g. This is similar to the force experienced when a racing car accelerates. What does the 'g' refer to?

23. *Shenzhou 5* is:

(i) a sportscar made in China.

(ii) a district in Shenzen in Southern China.

(iii) the name of the spacecraft which carried the first Chinese taikonaut.

iv) a factory which became famous for producing 5 million watches in a year.

24. This was the first space station of the United States and was in orbit from 1973 to 1979. In 1979, it re-

entered the Earth's atmosphere and the burnt debris came crashing to the ground, landing in Western Australia. What was the name of this space station?

25. *Rendezvous with Rama* is a work of science fiction in which a cylindrical space ship from interstellar space enters the solar system and is met by human beings who try to interact with the aliens in it. It was written by a famous author who is also credited with proposing satellite communications in 1945. Who is this author?

26. *Dialogue Concerning the Two Chief World Systems* is one of the most important books in the history of astronomy. In this, one of the protagonists, Salviati, argues for the validity of the Copernican heliocentric system while another, Simplicio, defends the Aristotelian geocentric view. Who wrote the book?

27. A series of treatises, written in ancient India in 1st Millenium BC, contain elaborate rules for the construction of fire altars for Vedic sacrifices. They also contain detailed discussions on Pythagorean numbers, geometry and algebra. Which books are these?

28. This civilisation in Central America used a calendar with a period of 260 days. The calendar also detailed the 584 day cycle of the planet Venus and is considered

to be very accurate. Which civilisation was this?

29. Dark Energy is:

(i) a form of energy which cosmologists think is present throughout the universe and is responsible for its accelerated expansion.

(ii) a form of energy found in dark underground caverns.

(iii) a form of energy used by ghosts and vampires.

(iv) energy which is emitted by a dark body.

30. Cygnus X-1 is one of the strongest X-ray sources that have been studied. It is estimated to be about 9 times as massive as our Sun in a very compact region. It was the first candidate for a class of astronomical objects which are hypothesised but never been directly observed. What are these objects?

MATHEMATICS

1. The Incas who ruled over most of South America from the 13th to the 16th century used an elaborate system of knotted ropes or strings for counting. What was this called?

2. The Babylonians were very accomplished mathematicians and clay tablets have been discovered which indicate that they could solve quadratic equations and evaluate roots of integers among other problems. The number system used by the Babylonians was base 60 (just like our own decimal number system is base 10) and in fact this has survived in our recording of time. What is this number system called?

3. The 'Sieve of Eratosthenes' is an algorithm devised by the Greek mathematician Eratosthenes. This algorithm is still one of the most efficient methods of solving a particular problem in number theory. What is the Sieve of Eratosthenes used for?

4. This book by Euclid has been hailed as one of the most important books in any subject of all times. The book contains theorems of geometry and till very recently, was required reading for all school children in the Western world. What is the name of the book?

5. This German mathematician laid the foundations of Set Theory and also formulated a theory of transfinite numbers, besides defining different kinds

of infinities. Who was he?

6. In 1976, Kenneth Apple and Wolfgang Haken proved a long standing conjecture in mathematics and cartography. Incidentally, this was the first major theorem to be proved using a computer. What was the name of the theorem?

7. In a speech to the International Congress of Mathematicians in 1900, a famous German mathematician listed 23 unsolved problems in mathematics which have remained the focus of most of mathematics till today. Who was the mathematician?

8. The 'Seven Bridges of Konigsberg' was a mathematical problem which was solved by a famous Swiss mathematician in 1735. He also did very significant work in mechanics and the motion of fluids. Who was this mathematician?

9. In 1796, the famous mathematician Gauss, showed that it was possible to construct a regular heptadecagon using only a compass and a ruler. That this can be done for regular polygons of 3, 4, 5, 6 sides, had been shown by Euclid. What is a heptadecagon?

10. This famous Greek philosopher was the first to enunciate the laws of logic as we know them. Who was he?

11. The systematic procedure which produces a result to a problem or an answer to a question in a finite number of steps is named after the Latinised version of the name of a 9th century Islamic scholar, Muhammad Ibn Musa al-Khwarizmi. What is such a procedure called?

(i) Algorithm

(ii) Algebra

(iii) Alchemy

(iv) Postulate

12. We know that counting numbers, that is positive integers, are called natural numbers. There are also numbers called rational numbers. What kind of numbers are these?

13. In Ancient Greece, followers of the famous mathematician Pythagoras studied positive numbers which have a curious property that the sum of their proper divisors is equal to the integer itself. For instance, 6 can be written as 6=3+2+1 or 28=14+7+4+2+1, etc. What are these numbers called?

14. In 1742, the Russian mathematician, Christian Goldbach, conjectured on an important property of all even numbers greater than 4. Goldbach's

conjecture is one of the oldest unsolved problems in mathematics. Though almost everyone believes it to be true, a rigorous proof is still not available. What is the conjecture?

15. The ancient Greeks believed that there were 5 Platonic Solids which served as the elementary constituents of solids in the universe. Which were the 5 Platonic Solids, 3-dimensional objects whose faces were regular polygons that meet each other at equal solid angles?

16. 'Wow, I made a great discovery' and 'Can I have a small container of coffee?' are two mnemonics which can be used to get the value of a very important number which is related to the ratio of the circumference and diameter of a circle. What is it?

17. We often use the term 'squaring the circle' to mean achieving the impossible. What does this phrase mean precisely in mathematics? And is it truly impossible?

18. One of the important kinds of prime numbers are Mersenne primes. What are these?

19. We know that a circle can be defined as the path on which every point is at a fixed distance from a fixed point called the centre of the circle. What figure is obtained in which every point is such that the sum of

the distance from two fixed points is a constant?

20. If a number p is a prime and p+2 is also a prime, what is the pair p and p+2 called?

21. An English mathematician and physicist and a German mathematician both claimed to have discovered calculus and had a long quarrel about who discovered it first. Ultimately, the matter was never resolved, though the notation that we use in calculus today owes itself to the German mathematician. Who were these two great mathematicians?

22. Arithmetic series is one in which the difference between successive terms is a constant. Thus, 1,3,5,7... is an example of an arithmetic series. What is a geometric series?

23. In 1913, the English philosopher, Bertrand Russel, and the mathematician, Alfred Whitehead, published a book which was supposed to have laid the foundation of mathematics. What was the name of the book?

24. Triangles with all three sides equal are called equilateral triangles while those with two sides equal are called isosceles triangles. What are triangles in which all three sides are different called?

25. I take an equilateral triangle and replace the middle third of each side with a bump so that the bump

itself forms an equilateral triangle with the missing segment. I repeat this process with every line segment and after many repetitions, I get a fascinating figure which is an example of a fractal. What is such a figure called?

26. When wind patterns and other weather factors are not relevant, most airline routes follow what are known as great circles. What is a great circle?

27. This famous Greek mathematician proved that the volume of a sphere is two-thirds that of the cylinder which just contains it (that is, having height and diameter equal to the diameter of the sphere).He was so proud of his achievement that he got it inscribed on his tomb! Who was the mathematician?

28. Perhaps the most famous theorem in mathematics is Fermat's last theorem. This was proposed by the French mathematician, Pierre Fermat, who intriguingly made a note in the margin saying he had found a proof which wouldn't fit in the margin! The theorem was finally proved in 1995 by an English mathematician. Who was he?

29. A little calculation! Here is one which deals with volumes—if a 12 cm in radius ball of lead weighs 32 kgs, what will be the weight of a 6 cm radius ball made from the same material?

30. The headquarters of Google, the famous search engine, was named after a very large number called googolplex. What is a googolplex?

31. Although we are used to space being flat, mathematicians have studied curved spaces where the usual rules of geometry as we know are not applicable. For instance, the sum of the angles of a triangle does not add up to 180 in curved space. In curved space, the shortest distance between two points is not the straight line but a path which is known as ________________.

32. We know that soap bubbles are approximately spherical in shape. This is not just a coincidence but because of a very special property of spheres. What is this property?

33. If we take a strip of paper and give it half a twist and join the ends together, we obtain a very interesting object which is also the subject of many lithographs by M.C. Escher. This object was first discovered by a German mathematician in the 19th century. What is this object?

34. A coffee mug and a doughnut are considered equivalent in this branch of mathematics. It is a field which finds many applications in physics and engineering and is popularly known as rubber sheet geometry. What is

this branch of mathematics called?

35. 'Reductio ad absurdum' is Latin for reduction to the absurd. It is a commonly used technique in mathematics. How is this technique used?

36. This French mathematician was the first to introduce coordinates and hence created the field of analytical geometry which allowed mathematicians to use algebraic techniques for geometry. The rectangular system of coordinates that we are familiar with are named after him. Who was he?

37. The Kepler conjecture is a mathematical conjecture first stated by the astronomer Johannes Kepler. It remained unsolved till 1998 when it was 'almost' solved by Thomas Hales. What is the conjecture?

38. The kissing number problem—we know that the maximum number of spheres that can simultaneously touch another sphere in two dimensions is 6. For three dimensions, the problem is not so easily solved and it was only in 1953 that the first correct proof was given. What is the number for three dimensions?

39. Although much better known as a poet, this 11th century Persian polymath did significant work in mathematics. Among the many problems he solved was finding the roots of a cubic equation using geometry. What was his name?

40. This 19th century book by Edwin Abbott Abbott, an English schoolteacher, although a satire on Victorian culture contained brilliant insights into how worlds in other than the normal 3 dimensions would function. It has been made into a film and has also been hailed by scientists as the best introduction to our understanding of lower dimensional worlds. What is the name of the book?

CHEMISTRY AND LIFE SCIENCES

1. In classical Hindu, Buddhist and Greek thought, the universe was made up of 5 elements. What are these elements?

2. This French chemist is called the Father of Modern Chemistry. Amongst his many achievements is the Law of Conservation of Mass which forms the basis of chemistry, compilation of a list of chemical elements and recognition of oxygen as an element. He was guillotined during the French Revolution. Who was he?

3. The first battery or chemical cell was made in 1800 by this Italian scientist. He is also credited with the discovery of methane from marsh gases and has been honoured in physics by an electricity unit being named after him. Who was the scientist?

4. In 1828, Friedrich Wohler, a German chemist, accidentally synthesised the first organic compound from inorganic chemicals. This proved to be a turning point in chemistry since it dealt a decisive blow to the popular vital force theory. What was the compound?

5. This Swedish chemist, who won the Nobel Prize in 1903, is best remembered for proposing the ionic theory. He is lesser known as the first person to have

proposed the greenhouse effect with increased carbon dioxide concentration in the atmosphere. Who was this scientist?

6. In 1869, a Russian chemist, Dimitri Mendeleev published the first periodic table by arranging the known elements in rows and columns according to their properties and structure. Using the periodic table he was able to predict the existence of many elements, two of whom he called eka-aluminum and eka-silicon. These elements were discovered later. Which elements are these?

7. The famous American chemist, Linus Pauling, is one of the two people who have won a Nobel Prize in two different fields. Which fields did Pauling get the Prizes in and who is the other person to have achieved this?

8. In 1939, Linus Pauling wrote a book which has been called the most influential book in chemistry. This book, which is still in print, changed the way chemistry was studied since it provided a quantum mechanical basis for it. What was the name of the book?

9. NMR spectroscopy is a major tool used by chemists to understand the structure of molecules, etc. What do the initials stand for?

10. We know that bioluminescence is the emitting of light by living organisms like fireflies. What is sonoluminescence?

11. We normally understand oxidation as the reaction of oxygen with a substance. However, in chemistry there is a more precise definition of oxidation which involves electrons. What is it?

12. This organic compound was first synthesised accidentally in 1938 and is now extensively used in industry and also for household utensils among other things. Its chemical name is Polytetrafluoroethylene (PTFE) but is better known as a brand name. What is the brand name?

13. *Aqua regia* from the Latin royal water is a chemical which is so reactive that it can dissolve gold. What is it?

14. The evocative sounding Piranha solution is another chemical reagent which is used to dissolve organic residues from vessels. What is it made of?

15. In 1918, this German scientist synthesised ammonia from nitrogen and hydrogen using a process which now bears his name. This was a very important development since ammonia is an important component of fertilisers and explosives. Prior to this, the only known source of nitrogenous compounds

was either organic, mostly guano (bird waste) or natural mineral deposits. What was the name of the scientist?

16. In 1952, Stanley Miller and Harold Urey performed a classic experiment which showed how life could have started on Earth. What did they do?

17. The 2009 Nobel Prize for chemistry was given to a chemist of Indian origin for his work on the structure and function of the ribosome. Who is the chemist?

18. This British chemist is the only person to have won two Nobel Prizes in chemistry. The first Prize in 1958 was for determining the amino acid sequence and structure of the protein insulin and the second Prize was for determining the DNA structure of an organism. What is the name of this remarkable scientist?

19. The chemical notations that we are familiar with now are only about 200 years old. They were invented by a Swedish chemist and pharmacist who used the first letters of the names of the elements to denote them. He however used superscripts for the numbers unlike the subscripts used now. Thus, for instance, water was H^2O rather than H_2O that we use today. What was the name of this doctor?

20. In 1865, a German chemist Kekule had a revolutionary idea which would prove to be of great importance in

organic chemistry. He is reported to have got the idea in a dream where he saw a snake biting its tail. What was the remarkable insight of Kekule?

21. Ernst Rutherford, a New Zealander working in England, performed a remarkable experiment in 1910. This experiment proved to be extremely important in understanding the structure of the atom but when confronted with the results, Rutherford was reported to have said, 'It is as if one hit a tissue paper with a 15 inch shell and it rebounded and came back at you'. What was he referring to?

22. The number of molecules in one mole of any substance is an enormous 6.02×10^{23}. What is this number called?

23. Till 1985, the element carbon was believed to have 3 forms or allotropes. Name them.

24. In 1985, a new allotrope of carbon was discovered where 60 atoms of carbon were arranged as if forming a soccer ball. This allotrope was named after an American architect. What is the name of this allotrope?

25. Carbon dating is a well known method which is used in archaeology to date the ages of biological samples like wood, bones, etc. Which isotope of carbon is used for carbon dating?

26. This is one of the few elements named after a country. It was discovered by Marie Curie and Pierre Curie in 1898. It was initially named Radium-F but the name changed later. Which element is this?

27. We know that chlorine gas is used to disinfect water—drinking water that is supplied by the municipality and the swimming pools smell of chlorine. What exactly is the chemical which kills the microorganisms in water when chlorine is mixed with water?

28. Why do some coloured clothes fade when left for a long time in sunlight?

29. What is the origin of the word limelight?

30. Sunscreen lotions prevent the skin from sunburns. How do they work?

31. Ascorbic acid, folic acid and pantothenic acid are extremely important substances for the human body. What are these chemicals ordinarily known as?

32. Limestone, chalk, calcite, marble and pearl are all different forms of the same chemical substance. Which substance is this?

33. In olden times, all physicians starting the practice of medicine were supposed to take an oath which bound them to behave ethically in their profession. This oath is believed to have been written by a Greek physician

in the 5th century BC. What is the oath called and who started it?

34. *Drosophila Melanogaster* is a well known organism which is used in biological experiments frequently since it reproduces in a very short time. What is the common name for this organism?

35. Malaria is one of the deadliest diseases known to humanity. Every year it kills hundreds of thousands of people. For a long time, the only cure for malaria was quinine. What is the origin of quinine?

36. This Austrian priest, in the late 19th century, carried out studies on the inheritance of various traits in pea plants and laid the foundations of the science of genetics. His work was not recognised in his lifetime but he gained fame after his death. Who was he?

37. In 1665, Robert Hooke, the famous English scientist was looking at thin slices of cork under a crude microscope when he saw many thin pores which resembled a honeycomb. What were these and what did he name them?

38. In biology, there are two kinds of cells—with nuclei and without nuclei. The cells with a nucleus are called eukaryotes. What are cells which do not have a nucleus called?

39. In most eukaryotic cells, almost all the energy

required by the cells is produced by a structure which is found in the cell outside the nucleus. What is this structure or organelle called?

40. Reproduction of eukaryotic cells takes place in two ways—either asexually or sexually. What are these two kinds of processes called?

41. The stomach is an important part of the digestive system. To aid the digestion of proteins, the stomach produces enzymes which can only work in an acidic environment. The stomach also produces an acid which serves the dual purpose of providing the acidic environment for the enzymes and also kills bacteria. What acid does the stomach produce?

42. For a long time it was believed that no bacteria would be able to survive or indeed live in the stomach because of the acidic environment. In the early eighties, two Australian scientists showed that not only does a particular bacterium, *Heliobacter pylori* survive in the stomach, it is also responsible for a deadly disease. What disease is this?

43. We know that DNA is the molecule which contains the genetic information in all living cells. The basic ingredient of DNA is a set of 4 bases which are attached to sugar and phosphate molecules. Which bases are these?

44. We know that the primary units of DNA are the bases which together with the sugar and phosphate molecules form a nucleotide. What are the basic units of a protein molecule?

45. In 1968, three scientists, including the Indian-born Hargobind Khorana got the Nobel Prize for their interpretation of the genetic code. What does one mean by the term genetic code?

46. PCR is a technique or a reaction which allows one to make millions of copies from a single DNA sequence in a short time. In fact, one can say that the whole biotechnology revolution would not have been possible without this single breakthrough. What is the full form of PCR?

47. In the history of the Earth, around 65 million years ago, a cataclysmic event occurred which is known as the Cretaceous-Tertiary extinction event. What happened to life on Earth due to this event?

48. We know that zoology is the branch of biology which deals with animals and botany deals with the plant kingdom. Within zoology, there are many sub-branches. What are ornithology and ichthyology?

49. Living organisms can survive in a host of environmental conditions. This is because their bodies can regulate their internal environment in such a way that the internal conditions remain unchanged despite drastic

changes in the external environment. This is done mostly by hormones. What is this property of living organisms called?

50. All living cells which use oxygen for respiration have a chemical cycle which is an essential part of metabolism to convert food into energy and carbon dioxide and other waste products. This cycle was discovered by a British biochemist and it got him the Nobel Prize in Medicine in 1953. What is this cycle known as and who was the biochemist who first discovered it?

51. Where in the human body is one likely to find the Islets of Langerhans?

52. Where in the human body are the red blood cells made and what is their typical lifespan? Which organs of the body are responsible for the degradation of the red blood cells after they die?

53. Which of the following diseases are not caused by a virus?

(i) Polio
(ii) Smallpox
(iii) Strep throat
(iv) Measles

54. *Curcumma Longa* is the botanical name for a plant of the ginger family which has been used for centuries in our country as a condiment. In addition, it has been used for

its medicinal properties as an antiseptic and for aches and pains. What is this plant commonly known as?

55. We have seen that geese and several other birds fly in a V shaped formation, much like fighter jets! Why do they fly in this particular formation?

56. Why do our eyes water when we chop onions?

57. Why do we sneeze if we inhale some pepper?

58. We have all heard that camels can travel in a desert for days without drinking water. How much water does a camel store in its hump?

59. The bark of the willow tree produces a chemical called salicylic acid which is very useful as a remedy for aches and pains and even fever. The earliest reference of its medicinal use is from the 5th century BC when the Greek physician Hippocrates wrote about the bitter powder obtained from the bark of a willow tree. What is this drug commonly called?

60. Why do our hands and feet get wrinkled when we immerse them in water for a long time?

61. Polio is one of the deadliest incurable diseases known to us. Prevention of polio is possible because of the development of the polio vaccine in the 1950s. Who were the scientists who developed the vaccine which has saved millions of lives worldwide?

TECHNOLOGY

1. One of the biggest revolutions in science was the development of logarithms in the 17th century. These allowed very difficult calculations, especially in surveying and astronomy, to be done easily. Who developed the first logarithmic tables?
2. In the early 17th century, William Oughtred, an English mathematician, invented a simple instrument which became indispensable for engineers and scientists till the advent of calculators. Most of us have probably never seen it but its use was universal till a few decades back. What was this instrument?
3. In 1801, this Frenchman invented a way to program textile looms by using a pack of punched cards which served as a template for intricate designs to be woven. This was an important step in conceptualising the idea of a programmable computer. Who was this Frenchman?
4. The first, general all-purpose computer was proposed in 1837 by the English mathematician and inventor, Charles Babbage, who is now regarded as the father of computers. What was the name of the device which he proposed, which never got built in his lifetime?
5. Though we use decimal notation (number system based on base 10) in our everyday lives, computers use a different number system. Which system do they use and what is the base?

6. Contrary to what is believed, the first program-controlled computer was not the ENIAC but a machine built by a German computer scientist, Konrad Zuse. What was this machine called?

7. In 1937, a brilliant English mathematician and logician, described a hypothetical machine which manipulates symbols on a moving paper tape and can compute any quantity which can be mathematically computed. This hypothetical machine played an important role in the development of computers. Who was the mathematician?

8. In 1989, some scientists working at the European Laboratory for Particle Physics, CERN, near Geneva needed a standard protocol to exchange data with their fellow workers. For this purpose they developed a protocol which paved the way for the World Wide Web. What was the protocol called?

9. The first browser which really allowed the web to be used by anyone was developed in 1993 by Marc Andreessen who later developed the browser program called Netscape. What was the name of the browser?

10. The invention of the Internet as we know it was made possible only with the development of a communication protocol in 1974. This protocol is

TCP, which was developed by Vincent Cerf and Robert Kahn. What is the full form of TCP?

11. Addresses of sites on the Internet are usually referred to as URLs. What is the full form of URL?

12. Most of us access the Internet through a telephone or a broadband connection using a modem. What is the full form of MODEM?

13. In 1958, Jack Kilby, an engineer, invented an electronic circuit which became the basis of all computers subsequently and indeed of all electronics. What was this device?

14. The first computer language to be used extensively was the language FORTRAN which was developed at IBM. What was the full form of FORTRAN?

15. C-programming language revolutionised the world of programming and has in fact become the most popular computer language in the world. Who invented C-programming language?

16. One of the earliest public key encryption programmes was developed in 1991 by Phil Zimmerman. It was called PGP. What is the full form of PGP?

17. All of us have seen USB drives which can carry a lot of data and fit into a USB port on the computer. What does USB stand for?

18. A patent for Cathode-Ray Tube Amusement Device was issued in the USA in 1948. What was the significance of this device?

19. In 1967, Doug Engelbart, the remarkable inventor, filed a patent for a device which was called 'X-Y position indicator for a display system'. This was a wooden box with two wheels. What is this device?

20. When the computer is booting, we frequently see BIOS settings. What is BIOS?

21. We all know of spreadsheet programmes like Microsoft Excel which help us in calculations and can perform various manipulations to numbers. Name the first spreadsheet program that was released in 1979 and became a big success.

22. The ancient Greek mathematician, Hero of Alexandria, describes an ingenious device which converted heat energy into mechanical energy. This device is called an aeolipile. What is this device?

23. One of the most important inventions of ancient Greece was a screw pump which consisted of a screw inside a hollow tube. This pump could be used to lift water and was very useful in irrigation. Which famous Greek mathematician and scientist invented this?

24. In 1498, Johannes Gutenberg invented the first

movable printing press. The first book printed on the press was printed in 1855. Name the book.

25. This 16th century Flemish cartographer first devised a way of projecting a globe on a flat surface, a projection which is still widely used and is known by his name. He was also the first person to coin the word 'Atlas' for a collection of maps. Who was he?

26. In 1701, an English agriculturist invented the seed drill which was a major step towards the mechanisation of agriculture. What was the name of this agriculturist? There is a very famous British rock band of the same name!

27. In 1837 John Deere, an American blacksmith, invented an agricultural implement which played an important role in the cultivation of the heavy prairie soil and hence paved the way for the development of the American West. What was this implement?

28. Otto von Guericke, a German engineer, carried out a famous demonstration in the German city of Magdeburg for his new invention. He harnessed 16 horses to a pair of hemispheres and tried to pull the hemispheres apart. What invention was he demonstrating?

29. The cotton gin was a very simple device invented

in 1793 which made possible the efficient removal of seeds from cotton fibre. This device, which was mechanised later, was largely responsible for the tremendous increase in the cultivation of cotton in America. Who was the inventor of the cotton gin?

30. In 1850, John Mercer, an English printer, invented a process which made it possible to colour cotton fabric with brighter and longer lasting colours. What is this process known as?

31. In 1888, a veterinary surgeon invented the pneumatic (air-filled) tyre for his son's bicycle. This invention, coming at the time when automobiles were being developed, played an important role in the popularity of the automobile for transport. Who was this surgeon?

32. In 1839, Charles Goodyear, an American, invented the process of vulcanisation of rubber which made natural rubber harder and more resistant to chemical attack. Vulcanised rubber is used in machinery and other goods. What is the element which is added to natural rubber during vulcanisation?

33. Although it is commonly believed that Remington invented the typewriter, the typewriter was invented by his business partner. What was the name of

the American inventor who got the patent for typewriters?

34. A major revolution in writing came with the development of fountain pens in 1884. For the first time, a pen could store ink and there was no more need for inkwells to dip the nib. Who was the inventor?

35. In 1867, the prolific American inventor, Edison, made the first phonograph using a stylus which made indentations on a thin material wrapped around a cylinder. What was the material?

36. One of the most important inventions for the development of radio communication was the triode. A triode was used to amplify the weak signals that were transmitted so as to make them detectable. Who invented the triode?

37. In 1865, a Scottish surgeon used the chemical carbolic acid on open wounds to control infections. This was the first use of chemical antiseptics which would ultimately save hundreds of millions of lives by preventing infections in wounds. A famous mouthwash is named after this surgeon! What was his name?

38. In 1895, the German scientist, Wilhelm Roentgen, accidentally discovered x-rays and realised its potential in medicine when he took the first x-ray.

What was the first x-ray image?

39. In 1908, Leo Baekeland, a Belgium-born chemist, patented a new material which was the first plastic to be used widely. It was used extensively in electrical equipment since it was a very good insulator. What was the name of this plastic?

40. The process for manufacturing steel from iron by adding carbon has been known for centuries. However, stainless steel, of the kind we use in utensils and other household objects, was made for the first time in 1913 by alloying an element with steel. Name the element.

41. The fungus *Penicillium notatum* has a very significant place in the history of medicine. What is significant about this particular fungus?

42. All cars being made in India now have very strict emission standards. This is achieved by using a catalytic converter in the car which is basically a honeycomb like structure through which the exhaust gases pass and are rendered less damaging. What is the catalyst inside a catalytic converter?

43. We have heard of night vision glasses which are used in the battlefield. How do they work?

44. We know that aluminium is a good conductor of heat.

Then how is it that when we wrap food in aluminium foil, it stays hot?

45. The compact disc player uses a laser to read information coded on a compact disc in the form of miniature ridges. What kind of radiation is produced by the laser in a CD player?

46. Batteries come in various sizes—C, D, AA, AAA, etc. However, all of them are rated at 1.5V. What is the difference between these batteries?

47. Why does the door of a microwave oven have a metallic mesh on the inside of the glass?

48. Ironing of cotton garments is usually done after sprinkling some water on them. Why?

49. Why is it that the range of AM radio signals is much more than FM radio signals?

50. What kind of light does the TV remote emit when in use? How does the TV know what action to take from the signal?

51. Who was the first person to have used mercury in a thermometer? He was also responsible for giving us a temperature scale.

52. Why does popcorn 'pop'?

53. How does a silencer or a muffler in a car reduce the noise?

54. What do the acronyms GSM and CDMA stand for in mobile phones?

55. We hear a lot about hybrid vehicles now. When was the first hybrid vehicle made and by whom?

56. Most hybrid cars nowadays use regenerative braking. What is this?

57. In 1958, Momofuku Ando of Japan introduced a convenience food which has been called the most important Japanese invention of the century! What was the product?

58. A crescograph is an instrument to measure the growth of plants. It was invented by a famous Indian scientist in the early 20th century. Who was the scientist?

59. In 1894, a patent was granted for a particular kind of food product made from maize. This product, named Granose initially, rapidly gained in popularity and is now used all over the world. What was this and who was the inventor?

60. All of us are familiar with MRI scans that have become very popular for diagnosing ailments. A very important part of a MRI scanner is a SQUID detector which measures very weak magnetic fields very accurately. What is the full form of SQUID?

ANSWERS

PHYSICS

1. The world's most powerful accelerator is the Large Hadron Collider (LHC) located near Geneva in Switzerland. The accelerator produces very high energy protons and antiprotons and studies their collisions. The LHC is a modern day engineering marvel. The accelerator lies in a tunnel, 27 km in circumference, at a depth of about 100 m below ground. The accelerator has over 1600 superconducting magnets, and uses about 100 tonnes of liquid helium to maintain a temperature of about -270°C. The accelerator consumes about 120 MW of power which is what a medium-sized city would consume! At a cost of $9 billion, this is the most expensive scientific project ever undertaken by humans.
2. The Higgs particle, named after the English physicist Peter Higgs who in 1965 predicted the existence of this particle.
3. Quarks are particles which were proposed by Murray Gell-Mann in 1961. He took the name from a nonsensical rhyme in James Joyce's *Finnegan's Wake*—"three quarks for Muster Mark".
4. Quantum Chromodynamics is the theory to explain a kind of fundamental force, the strong force which is experienced by nuclear particles. The 'chromo' refers to the colour charge— a quantity which, like the electrical charge, is an inherent property of the quarks, the fundamental constituents of nuclear particles.

5. (iii) Einstein was awarded the Nobel Prize for his theory which explained the photoelectric effect. This is the phenomenon when electrons are emitted from certain materials when light falls on them.

6. Enrico Fermi developed the first nuclear reactor in 1942. The man-made element, Fermium, is named after him, as are fermions, which are elementary particles. The Fermi National Accelerator Laboratory near Chicago is also named in his honour.

7. (iv) The Manhattan Project was the codename for the project based in Los Alamos, New Mexico, in the United States during the World War II for the development of the Atomic Bomb.

8. John Dalton, who developed the atomic theory, was colour blind. Daltonism is the common term for colour blindness.

9. Positronium. Although it had been predicted for many years, it was first observed in 1951.

10. There are 92 natural elements known to us and Uranium is the heaviest natural element. However, scientists have produced elements heavier than Uranium in the laboratory. In fact, there are now 117 elements known to us, including 25 that are produced in the laboratory.

11. J. Robert Oppenheimer.

12. Erwin Schrodinger.

13. Helium was first seen as a line in the solar spectrum and is named after 'helios'—the Greek word for Sun. Helium is the most abundant element in the universe after hydrogen.

14. (ii) Helium. Adding a neutron to a nucleus doesn't change the element. Adding neutrons to an element increases the atomic weight but not the atomic number. Different forms of the same element with differing atomic weights are called isotopes.

15. (ii) According to the quantum theory, when electrons fall from a higher energy state to lower energy states, they emit electromagnetic energy which is exactly equal to the difference in the energies of the two states. In case this energy corresponds to the visible spectrum, one gets light.

16. The curved shape of the base of aluminium cans provides greater structural stability to the can in much the same way as a dome in a building. Furthermore, in the case of aerosol spray cans, it makes it easier to use up the last bit of the fluid in the can.

17. Daniel Bernoulli first proposed what is now known as Bernoulli's Principle. This principle is a relationship between the speed of a fluid, its potential energy and the pressure.

18. The time period of a pendulum is proportionate to the square root of the length. Hence if the time period of a pendulum of length 4 feet is 2 seconds, a pendulum of length 1 foot will have a time period of 1 second.

19. (ii) Newton was appointed the Master of the Royal Mint in 1696, an office he retained till his death in 1727.

20. Blaise Pascal invented the hydraulic press and gave Pascal's Law in hydrostatics. He got interested in probability because of his friend who was a gambler and together with Fermat, developed the fundamentals of probability science.

21. All three are examples of a simple machine—the lever. A crowbar is an example of a Class 1 lever, a wheelbarrow of Class 2 and the elbow joint of Class 3 lever.

22. Gaspart-Gustave Coriolis first studied the direction of flow of air in a cyclone in relation to the hemisphere, and the effect is known as Coriolis effect.

23. Gyroscope. The first use of a gyroscope to study the rotation of the Earth was by the French mathematician Foucault who also gave it this name from the Greek words for Earth and 'to see'.

24. Ball bearings greatly reduce friction among moving parts since sliding friction (in the absence of ball bearings) is much more than rolling friction with ball bearings.

25. Differential gears are used to change the direction of motion. This is the sphere-like structure you see between the two rear wheels of most trucks and buses.

26. Velocity. This is Newton's Second Law of Motion which states that the product of the mass and acceleration is the external force. Since the rate of change of velocity is the acceleration, this is just another way to state the Second Law.

27. (iii) The length of totality in the solar eclipse depends on the position of the Moon in its orbit and the maximum duration for totality is 7 minutes and 31 seconds.

28. The light from the Sun, which is mostly blocked by the disc of the Moon, passes through the valleys on the surface of the Moon, giving the appearance of bright spots of light shining like beads.

29. (i) Lunar eclipse occurs when the Moon passes through

the Earth's shadow and thus can only happen when it is on the far side of the Earth from the Sun.

30. Rheology is the study of viscosity.

31. Isaac Newton. The reflecting telescope is usually called a Newtonian reflector.

32. True. The main ingredient in glass as well as sand or quartz is silicon dioxide or silica. Although it is possible to make glass from silica alone, usually other chemicals are added to simplify the manufacture. But the primary material in glass is silica.

33. Edwin Land.

34. Phase contrast microscopy. In this, the change in the properties of light (phase) passing through a transparent sample are converted to changes in contrast. Since most biological specimens are transparent, they can be viewed with this without staining to make them opaque as in a regular optical microscope.

35. MASER (Microwave Amplification by Stimulated Emission of Radiation) preceded the development of lasers which give out visible light. In fact, when the first laser was made, it was called an optical MASER!

36. The product of frequency and wavelength of any wave gives us the speed of the wave. For light travelling in vacuum, the speed of light is a constant, usually denoted by c and has a value of 299,792,458 m per second.

37. The retina. These are the three classes of photoreceptors which allow all vertebrates to sense light and convert it into nerve impulses to be interpreted by the brain. For many years, it was thought that there were only two

kinds of photoreceptors, rods and cones. In the 1990s, photosensitive ganglion cells were discovered which also perform the same function.

38. Total internal reflection of sunlight within the water droplets and the dispersion of light by the raindrops leads to the formation of a rainbow.

39. Sound waves are longitudinal pressure waves in which the disturbance is in the same direction as the direction of the motion of the wave. Longitudinal waves, unlike transverse waves, cannot be polarised.

40. 20 cycles per second to 20,000 cycles per second.

41. The Mach number of an object is the speed of the object in a substance divided by the speed of sound in that substance. The speed of sound at 15°C in the atmosphere is about 1225 km/hr. Mach numbers between 1 and 5 are called supersonic while those above 5 are termed as hypersonic.

42. An adiabatic process is one in which no heat is exchanged between the system and the surroundings.

43. Average kinetic energy. The higher the kinetic energy of the particles in any system, the higher is the temperature.

44. -273.15°C is the minimum temperature attainable. A more common scale of temperature used in physics is degrees Kelvin whose zero is defined as -273.15°C. Thus the boiling point of water on this scale is 373.15K.

45. No. For any heat engine, there is a limit to the efficiency which comes from the laws of thermodynamics. This limit depends on the temperature and cannot be exceeded

by any engine. Sadi Carnot, a French engineer, first gave this limit in the form of a theorem called Carnot's Theorem.

46. The Second Law of Thermodynamics or the Law of Increasing Entropy. Another way to say this is that any isolated system always goes from a more orderly state to a less orderly state.

47. Elektron is the Greek word for amber. It had long been known that amber and other resins, when rubbed, could attract other objects. This phenomenon was studied by William Gilbert in the 16th century who also coined the word.

48. Luigi Galvani. Galvanometer, an instrument to detect current, is named in his honour.

49. Diamagnetic substances are repelled by the magnetic field. Examples of diamagnetic materials are bismuth, antimony, zinc, etc.

50. Alternating, Direct. The current from the electric mains in our house is alternating current or AC while the current obtained from a torchlight battery or a mobile phone battery is direct current or DC.

51. Piezoelectric effect is the generation of electric current when certain kinds of crystals like quartz are deformed. In quartz watches, a tiny battery supplies the current to deform the crystals in a regular fashion to provide a measure of time.

52. A tetrode has four electrodes. Triodes (with 3 electrodes) and Pentodes (with 5 electrodes) were used before the advent of transistors for amplification of weak signals.

53. An internal combustion engine burns fuel inside the engine and uses the hot gases to power the engine. An external combustion engine burns fuel outside the engine and then uses the hot gases or liquids to power the engine. Automobile engine, whether petrol or diesel is an internal combustion engine, while a steam engine is an external combustion engine.

54. Terminal velocity. Any object falling in a medium experiences a drag or frictional force which increases with the speed of the object. Hence, when a parachutist jumps off, his speed increases due to gravity and so does the drag force due to air resistance. At some point, the two forces balance out and the resulting constant speed is called terminal velocity.

55. The dimples on a golf ball create a symmetrical turbulent boundary layer on the ball. This is responsible for more stable trajectories of the ball.

56. (iii) Ultrasound is typically any sound which is higher than the human audible range. The audible range of sound is 20 hertz-20 kilohertz. Ultrasound is frequency greater than 20 kilohertz.

57. About 91.7% of the ice cube is below the water. The same is roughly true for icebergs except that the density of sea water is different from 1 gm/cc because of dissolved salts.

58. The fundamental is the note of the lowest frequency (longest wavelength) that is produced by an instrument. In this case, the longest wavelength of a standing wave on the string will be twice the length of the string—50 cm.

59. A shotput, once it is thrown, is an example of projectile

motion and follows a parabolic path. The maximum range or horizontal distance is achieved by throwing it at an angle of 45 to the horizontal.

60. When electric power is transmitted across large distances, there is an energy loss due to the resistance of the transmission cables. This loss is much less when the voltage is high, hence electric power is transmitted at high voltages and then brought down to low voltage in the substations with the help of transformers.

ASTRONOMY AND SPACE SCIENCE

1. Nicolaus Copernicus. Copernicus' book contained his revolutionary heliocentric theory about the motion of heavenly bodies.
2. Active Galactic Nuclei—these are compact regions near the centre of some galaxies which emit much more radiation than the normal galaxy. These are regions where scientists think that super-massive black holes exist.
3. Kuiper Belt. It is named after the Dutch astronomer, Gerard Kuiper, who in 1951 proposed the existence of such a region beyond Neptune.
4. Oort Cloud is believed to contain trillions of small objects of size around 1 km which are mostly made up of frozen water, carbon monoxide, methane, etc. It is also believed that there might be some rocky objects in the cloud.
5. 220 km/sec is the speed of the Sun in its revolution

around the galactic centre which it completes once in 225–250 million years.

6. Ganymede revolves around Jupiter and has a radius of about 2600 km making it slightly larger than Mercury. Ganymede is named after the Greek mythological prince who was abducted by Zeus (Jupiter).

7. Olympus Mons is located on Mars and has been known to astronomers since the 19th century. It is a volcano with gentle sloping sides.

8. Mercury. A Mercury day is about two Mercury years long and its distance from the Sun varies from 46 to 70 million km making it the most eccentric orbit in the solar system.

9. The Cassini Division is a region about 4800 km wide between Ring A and Ring B of the planet Saturn. It was believed to be empty but it is now known to have a thinly distributed material similar to the rings.

10. Jupiter. Due to its huge gravitational pull, it receives the maximum number of cometary impacts of any planet in the solar system.

11. The planet Uranus, though it had been observed by the ancient astronomers, was never thought to be a planet because it was too dim and slow moving.

12. Karl Jansky accidentally discovered radio waves coming from outer space when he was investigating transatlantic voice communications at Bell Laboratories.

13. (ii) COBE (Cosmic Microwave Background Explorer) was a satellite launched in 1989 to study the radiation that permeates the universe and is thought to have originated in the very early epochs of the history of the universe.

14. Fraunhofer lines were named after the German optician Joseph von Fraunhofer. They provide information about the Sun's composition.

15. Sirius.

16. Sirius B is a white dwarf star. These are stars which start off like our Sun but which have exhausted all their nuclear fuel and have become very small and compact. Interestingly, it was the Indian-American scientist, S. Chandrasekhar, who worked out the correct theory for the white dwarfs in 1931.

17. Brahamagupta. The *Brahmasputhsiddhanta* was a major text on mathematics and astronomy and in fact it was only through this work that the Arab astronomers came to know about the Indian astronomical tradition.

18. Supernovae explosions.

19. Edwin Hubble who in 1929 discovered the relationship between distance and velocity. Hubble's Law, as this relationship is now known, is one of the fundamental tenets of cosmology.

20. The General Theory of Relativity which was propounded by Einstein in 1915. The amount of bending of light by objects as predicted by this theory was in concurrence with what Eddington measured in 1919.

21. (i) The *V2* rocket which was developed during World War II was the first object to reach into space.

22. 'g' refers to the acceleration due to gravity at the surface of the Earth, which is 9.8 m/s. A force of 5g is the force equivalent to 49 Newtons per kg of mass.

23. (iii) China launched its first human spaceflight mission

in 2003 with the *Shenzhou 5* spacecraft.

24. Skylab. Salyut, the first station to be put into orbit in 1971, was launched by Russia.

25. Arthur C. Clarke first proposed geostationary satellites of the kind used for communications in 1945. His most famous book is *2001: A Space Odyssey* which was also made into a famous film by Stanley Kubrick.

26. Galileo wrote this book in 1632 as a defence of the Copernican system. This book was placed in the 'Index of Forbidden Books' by the Church and Galileo was accused of heresy. The book was removed from the Index only in 1835!

27. The *Shulba Sutras* which are among the most important sources of information about the development of mathematics in Ancient India.

28. The Mayan civilisation which prospered in the highland areas of Guatemala and Mexico in the 3rd-10th century AD. The Mayan calendar was a refinement of the traditional calendar which was in use in the region from at least the 6th century BC.

29. (i) Dark energy is a hypothetical energy which physicists think is present in the universe and is one of the explanations for an accelerating expansion of the universe.

30. Cygnus X-1 was the first candidate for a black hole. These are objects which are so dense and hence have such a strong gravitational force that not even light can escape from them. All evidence accumulated about Cygnus X-1 since its discovery in 1964 points towards it being a black hole.

MATHEMATICS

1. Quipu, which consisted of coloured llama hair spun or threaded together in which the knots could be used to store numerical data, were used for counting by the Incas.

2. Sexagesimal.

3. The Sieve of Eratosthenes is an algorithm which can be used to find all the prime numbers upto a particular integer. It is still used since it is very efficient for values upto about 10 million.

4. *Elements* by Euclid which laid the foundation of mathematics as we know it now. In addition to the well-known theorems of Euclid, it also contained results in number theory.

5. Georg Cantor.

6. The Four Colour Theorem which states that contiguous regions which share a border on a plane can be coloured using at most 4 colours in such a way that no two adjacent regions are of the same colour.

7. David Hilbert proposed the problems which have come to be known as Hilbert's problems. Out of these, only 10 have been solved while 7 are partially solved.

8. Leonhard Euler was the first to show that the Seven Bridges of Konigsberg had a negative solution. Euler is also remembered for his work on the motion of rigid bodies and also fluids.

9. A heptadecagon is a 17-sided polygon.

10. Aristotle. Although there were discussions of logic in ancient Indian and Chinese texts, it was the work of Aristotle that laid the foundations of modern mathematics and science.

11. (i) Algorithm.

12. Rational numbers are those which can be expressed as a ratio of two integers. There are some numbers, appropriately called irrational numbers, which cannot be expressed as such. An example, well known to the ancient Indian mathematicians as far back as the 8th century BC is the square root of 2 or $\sqrt{2}$ which is the size of the diagonal of a square with side 1 unit and cannot be expressed as a fraction.

13. Perfect numbers.

14. Goldbach's conjecture states that any even number greater than 4 can be written as a sum of two primes.

15. The pyramid (4 faces), cube (6 faces), octahedron (8 faces), dodecahedron (12 faces) and icosahedron (20 faces).

16. These are mnemonics to get the value of π (3.14159.., 3.1415926...)

17. 'Squaring the circle' means constructing a square whose area is exactly equal to the area of a given circle using only a compass and a straight edge or a ruler. This was one of the problems which fascinated the Greeks and many Greek mathematicians tried to do it but failed. It has now been shown to be impossible to do.

18. Mersenne primes are primes of the form 2n – 1. Only

44 Mersenne primes are known and the largest primes are invariably Mersenne primes. Examples of the first few primes are obtained for n=2,3,5, namely, 3,7,31. Although known to early mathematicians like Euclid, they are named after the 17th century French monk, Marin Mersenne, who compiled a list of such primes.

19. An ellipse. The sum of the distance from two fixed points—called the foci of the ellipse—is a constant. Planets revolve around the Sun in elliptical orbits with the Sun as one of the foci.

20. Twin primes. For instance, 3 and 5, 11 and 13 are twin primes.

21. Sir Isaac Newton and Gottfried Liebniz, both of whom claimed to have been the first to have discussed calculus.

22. A geometric series is one in which the ratio of successive terms is a constant. Thus 2,4,8,16.... is an example of a geometric series with a common ratio of 2.

23. *Principia Mathematica*. Although this book formalised all the known mathematical theories, it turned out to be not too popular because of its complexity.

24. Scalene triangles.

25. Koch snowflake. It was first described in 1904 by the Swedish mathematician H. Koch.

26. A great circle on a sphere is one which cuts the sphere into two equal halves. The centre of a great circle is the centre of the sphere itself. The shortest distance between two points on the surface of a sphere is along the great circle connecting them.

27. Archimedes. It is said that Archimedes was solving a geometrical problem when he was attacked by Roman soldiers. He requested them to not disturb him which enraged them so much that they killed him.

28. Andrew Wiles. Fermat's theorem had defied proof for over three centuries until Wiles proved it after eight years of struggling with the proof.

29. Four kg. This is because the volume of the sphere is proportional to the cube of the radius. Thus, a sphere with one half the radius has one eighth the volume and one eighth the weight since the material (and hence the density) of the two balls is the same.

30. A googolplex is a number which is 1 raised to the power of 10^{100} zeroes. This is vastly greater than the number of elementary particles believed to exist in the universe!

31. Geodesic. A geodesic on the surface of a sphere for instance, is the arc of a great circle.

32. Spheres have a property that of all the solids having a given volume, the sphere is the one with the smallest surface area. Also, for a given surface area, the sphere has the greatest volume. For a soap bubble, the volume is fixed and the surface tension of the soap film tends to contract the bubble to the minimum surface area possible, which is that of a sphere.

33. Mobius strip. A Mobius strip has an interesting property that it is a surface with only one side and is non-orientable.

34. Topology. This is the branch where two objects are considered equivalent if they can be transformed into one another by bending, shrinking, twisting, etc. without

tearing apart or joining together. Thus, a coffee mug can be transformed into a doughnut and so they are equivalent topologically.

35. 'Reductio ad absurdum' is basically proof by contradiction. It is used widely in proving mathematical propositions where the opposite of what needs to be proved is taken to be true and then analysed to show how it leads to an absurd contradiction, thereby showing that the proposition itself must be true.

36. Rene Descartes, after whom the Cartesian coordinate system is named, was the first to create the field of analytical geometry.

37. The Kepler conjecture is a statement that no arrangement of equally-sized spheres filling space has a greater average density than that of the cubic close packing and hexagonal close packing arrangements. These are arrangements whose density is slightly more than 74%. In fact, if one randomly drops equal sized spheres into a container, then the average density obtained is about 65%. Hales showed that no matter how carefully one arranges the spheres, the density cannot be more than about 74%.

38. The maximum number of spheres that can simultaneously touch another sphere in three dimensions is 12. Newton had conjectured correctly that it was 12 but gave no concrete proof for his conjecture.

39. Omar Khayyam, who is well known as the author of *Rubaiyat*. He wrote an important treatise on algebra and also studied the parallel postulate of Euclid.

40. *Flatland* which was written in 1884 and made into a film in 2007.

CHEMISTRY AND LIFE SCIENCES

1. Earth, Fire, Water, Air and Aether. In Greek thought, Aether was added as an element by Aristotle.
2. Antoine Lavoisier.
3. Alessandro Volta who developed the first chemical cell to produce electricity, thereby founding the whole field of electrochemistry. The unit of electric potential, Volt, is named in his honour.
4. Wohler accidentally synthesised urea when he was trying to make ammonium cyanate. Urea had previously been isolated as a constituent of urine and hence was thought to be organic.
5. Svante Arrhenius, who proposed the ionic theory as part of his PhD thesis. He also proposed a theory of the formation of ice ages and speculated about the greenhouse effect caused by carbon dioxide.
6. Eka-aluminum is now known as gallium, while eka-silicon is germanium.
7. Pauling was awarded the Nobel Prize in Chemistry in 1954 and the Nobel Peace Prize in 1962. The only other person to have got Nobel Prizes in two different fields is Marie Curie who got it in Physics (1903) and Chemistry (1911).
8. *The Nature of the Chemical Bond* was based on Pauling's work on chemical bonding and fetched him the Nobel Prize in Chemistry.
9. Nuclear Magnetic Resonance spectroscopy. In this, the

magnetic properties of certain nuclei are used to extract information about the structure of the substances.

10. Sonoluminescence is the emission of light by bubbles in a liquid when they implode under the action of sound waves.

11. Oxidation is defined as the loss of electrons by a molecule, atom or ion. Similarly, reduction (the opposite of oxidation) is defined as the gain of electrons.

12. Teflon, which is used to make non-stick cookware because it is non-reactive.

13. *Aqua regia* is made up of 1 part concentrated nitric acid and 3 parts concentrated hydrochloric acid. Apart from gold, it can dissolve platinum too but strangely, does not react with titanium.

14. Piranha solution is concentrated sulphuric acid and hydrogen peroxide mixed in a ratio of 3:1. It is used in the chip industry as a solvent and as the name suggests is very dangerous.

15. Fritz Haber, together with Carl Bosch, developed the process to use hydrogen and atmospheric nitrogen to synthesise ammonia. The process is called the Haber process or the Haber-Bosch process.

16. They took a mixture of water, methane, ammonia and hydrogen (all the chemicals present on Earth before life is supposed to have begun) in a flask and passed an electric spark to simulate lightning. At the end of the experiment they found the presence of amino acids (from which proteins can be formed) in the flask thus showing how life could have begun on Earth.

17. Venkatraman Ramakrishnan.

18. Fredrick Sanger.
19. Jons Jacob Berzelius, who also identified several elements like silicon and thorium.
20. Kekule proposed a ring like structure for the aromatic organic liquid ring shape structure which was extremely important in the development of organic chemistry.
21. Rutherford was shooting alpha particles on thin gold foils. Though as was expected, most of the alpha particles went right through the foil, at least some of them recoiled back. This was completely contrary to what the idea of atomic structure was at that time.
22. Avogadro's number, which is named after the famous French chemist Amedeo Avogadro.
23. Amorphous carbon, graphite and diamond—each having hugely different physical properties.
24. Fullerene which is named in honour of Buckminster Fuller, the polymath architect who designed the geodesic dome. The fullerene molecule resembles the geodesic dome.
25. Carbon-14 which is present in trace quantities in the atmosphere and is assimilated by living organisms in the form of carbon dioxide which is used by plants to make food. Carbon-14, unlike the normal carbon-12 isotope is radioactive and decays over time.
26. Polonium which was named in honour of Poland, the native country of Marie Curie.
27. Chlorine gas dissolves in water and forms hypochlorous acid (HOCl) which is a weak acid. This acid dissociates in water to form hypochlorite ions which are responsible for killing the microorganisms.

28. Sunlight, apart from the visible part of the spectrum, also has an ultraviolet component. The ultraviolet light is very energetic and when it interacts with the dye molecules which are responsible for the colour, they tend to dissociate causing the colour to fade.

29. When quicklime is heated to 2400 °C, it emits an intense glow. This form of illumination is known as limelight and was used in theatrical productions prior to the invention of electric lighting.

30. Sunburns are usually caused by the energetic ultraviolet part of sunlight. Sunscreen lotions have certain kinds of chemicals which absorb the ultraviolet light, in the same manner as fluorescent materials do. However, unlike fluorescent materials which reemit the energy absorbed as light, sunscreen chemicals reemit the energy as heat which is not particularly harmful to the skin.

31. Vitamin C, Vitamin B9 and Vitamin B5, all of which are extremely important for preventing deficiency diseases.

32. Calcium carbonate.

33. The Hippocratic oath, named after Hippocrates who is considered to be the father of western medicine.

34. The common fruit fly. It is used for many biological experiments since the time taken for the development of an egg to a mature individual is only about a week.

35. Quinine was derived from the bark of the cinchona tree which was native to the Andes. In fact, the Quechua people of Peru had used the bark for centuries as a treatment for fever. In the 17th century, the Jesuit priests brought back the bark to Europe and its use became

widespread as an antidote to malaria.

36. Gregor Mendel who studied more than 25,000 pea plants and formulated the laws of genetics which now form the basis of our understanding of the field.

37. Hooke saw the cells in the cork slices and in fact he was the first person to call them cells since they resembled the cells in a honeycomb.

38. Prokaryotes—all bacteria belong to this category.

39. Mitochondria. Apart from producing most of the cell's energy, these also play a role in cell reproduction, ageing and regulation.

40. Asexual reproduction or mitosis is the process whereby the parent cell divides into two identical daughter cells which can further divide. In sexual reproduction or meiosis, the cell cannot divide till it is fertilised and then its genetic material is replicated and two daughter cells are produced.

41. Hydrochloric acid.

42. Peptic ulcer which is an ulcer of the stomach lining. *Heliobacter pylori* have been shown to be one of the major causes of stomach ulcers.

43. The DNA molecule is a long, helical arrangement of 4 bases—Adenine (A), Cytosine(C), Guanine (G) and Thymine (T).

44. Amino acids. There are 22 standard amino acids which bind together in specific ways to make all the proteins that are required by the organism.

45. The basic function of the DNA is to provide the sequence in which the amino acids join up to form a particular

protein. The arrangement of triplets of the bases in the DNA (called codons) determines which amino acid is in what position in the protein. This mapping between the triplet of bases and the amino acids is called the genetic code.

46. Polymerase Chain Reaction which was discovered by Kary Mullis in 1983. It uses an enzyme, DNA polymerase, to synthesise many copies of the DNA from a single strand. Mullis got a Nobel Prize for this work in 1993.

47. The Cretaceous-Tertiary extinction event was responsible for the extinction of most dinosaurs. Opinion among the scientists is divided on what caused the event. The causes of the extinction range from impact of an asteroid to volcanic eruptions.

48. Ornithology is a branch of zoology that involves the study of birds. Salim Ali was the most famous ornithologist in India. Ichthyology is the study of fishes.

49. Homeostasis. This is an important characteristic of all living organisms and allows them to survive in adverse environmental conditions temporarily.

50. The Kreb's cycle or the citric-acid cycle. This was discovered by Hans Krebs in 1937.

51. Islets of Langerhans are the regions of the pancreas which were first identified in 1829 by a German pathologist. These regions contain the cells which produce the all important hormone insulin which converts glucose into fat.

52. Red blood cells are made in the bone marrow and live for about 100-120 days. The degradation is mostly carried out in the spleen and the liver.

53. Strep throat which is caused by the deadly bacteria *Streptococcus pyogenes*. The other diseases are caused by viral infections.

54. Turmeric or haldi. Turmeric has a chemical, Curcumin, which has anti bacterial properties and hence is useful as an antiseptic.

55. Geese and other migrating birds have to fly long distances to reach more hospitable environments. Flying in a V-shaped formation serves two purposes. One, it conserves energy since each bird flies slightly higher than the bird in front and hence encounters less air resistance. Secondly, it is much easier to keep track of each other in this formation since communication and coordination is easier. It is primarily for this second reason that fighter jets fly in this formation.

56. Our eyes have a type of gland called lachrymal which produce tears. Onions release a chemical called syn-propanethial-S-oxide which irritates the lachrymal glands and they produce tears. It has recently been found that the actual process of release of this chemical irritant is quite complicated and involves several enzymes and other chemicals.

57. Sneezing is a reflex action of the nose to get rid of unwanted objects. The membrane inside the nose gets irritated by piperine, a chemical which is found in pepper. The irritation of the membrane in the nose induces this reflex action of sneezing. Incidentally, when one sneezes, air rushes out of the nose at a phenomenal 150 km an hour!

58. None! Camels store the water in their bloodstream. They store fat in their humps and this fat is used as a source

of energy when the camels do not find food to eat.

59. Aspirin which is acetylsalicylic acid. Aspirin was first synthesised in 1853, though the use of salicylic acid as a medicine had been known for centuries.

60. The wrinkling of the hands and feet is because the outermost layer of cells on our skin has dead keratin cells. When in water for long, these absorb water and swell up. This layer is attached to the layer of living cells underneath and to compensate for the increased area of the swollen cells, the skin wrinkles. The reason why this happens only on the hands and feet is because the hands and feet have the thickest layer of keratin which is required since the skin on the palms and feet needs to be tougher than other parts of tne body.

61. The first effective polio vaccine was developed by Jonas Salk in 1952. This was an injectible vaccine which was made from an inactivated polio virus. Subsequently, Albert Sabin developed an oral form of the vaccine which has since been in use throughout the world. The oral polio vaccine uses an attenuated polio virus.

TECHNOLOGY

1. John Napier, a Scottish mathematician and astrologer, who in 1614, published the first set of logarithm tables in his book, *Mirifici Logarithmorum Canonis Descriptio*.

2. Slide rule. Based on logarithmic tables, this simple device allowed quick calculations and was used extensively by engineers and scientists. It is basically a mechanical

computer which is however analogue and not digital.

3. Joseph Jacquard. He invented the Jacquard loom which could be programmed to weave different patterns by the use of a stack of programmable paper cards.

4. The Analytical Engine. Though the machine never got built during Babbage's lifetime, his son built one partially in 1910.

5. Computers use binary arithmetic where the base, instead of being 10 as in decimal mathematics that we are familiar with, is 2. Thus, in binary notation, the number 2 is represented by 10 while 10 is represented by 1010.

6. Zuse Z3 was built in 1941 and used film reels instead of punched cards for storing the program.

7. Alan Turing proposed what is now called a Turing Machine. Turing was also responsible for cracking the ENIGMA code which was being used by the Nazis.

8. HTTP—HyperText Transfer Protocol. This one invention by Tim Berners-Lee and his co-workers standardised how computers communicated with servers and hence was crucial to the development of the World Wide Web.

9. Mosaic—this browser allowed users to point and click, thereby making the use of browsers easy for anyone with a computer.

10. Transmission Communication Protocol which allows different machines on a network to assemble and transmit data.

11. Uniform Resource Locator. This is the address one types in the browser to access the site- for instance, http://www.google.com

12. MOdulator-DEModulator (Modem) is a device which basically allows us to code digital information from a computer to send over telephone wires.

13. Integrated Circuit or a silicon chip. This is basically a miniaturised electronic circuit which has been made directly on a thin wafer of silicon or some other semiconducting material.

14. FORmula TRANslating system was the name of the language which was developed at IBM. This language quickly became popular with scientists and engineers and is in fact still the most widely used language for scientific programming.

15. Dennis Ritchie developed C-programming language in 1972 while working at the Bell Laboratories. The language was initially intended to be used for the UNIX operating system.

16. Pretty Good Privacy.

17. Universal Serial Bus. This is a specification developed so that devices could communicate with the controller which is in the computer. Thus we have USB printers, hard drives or other peripherals.

18. This was the design of the first video game where with the help of 8 vacuum tubes and a cathode-ray tube (like the display in old computer monitors) one could simulate a missile hitting a target.

19. The computer mouse! Engelbart christened it a mouse since it had a wire sticking out at the back, just like a mouse! Engelbart also played a significant role in developing GUI (Graphical User Interface)—the precursor to Windows.

20. Basic Input/Output System. This is the standard code which is run on a PC when it boots up.

21. VisiCalc, which was first released to run on an Apple II computer and became hugely popular with the users.

22. An Aeolipile is the first recorded example of a steam engine in which steam drives a body. It was described by Hero in 1st century AD though it is believed to be of ancient origin.

23. Archimedes. The screw pump, which was in continuous use in irrigation for over two millennia, is also known as Archimedes Screw.

24. The first book printed using Gutenberg's press was the Vulgate *Bible*. This had 3 volumes and had no page numbers or title page.

25. Gerardus Mercator whose projection, now known as the Mercator projection, proved to be very useful for navigation.

26. Jethro Tull.

27. A plough made from steel. The soil of the American prairies, though immensely productive was very hard to till since it was heavy. The introduction of the steel plough made extensive cultivation possible in the prairies.

28. The vacuum pump which Guericke invented in 1650. To demonstrate it, he took two hemispheres and removed the air between them using his pump and then tried to get them to be pulled apart by using 16 horses.

29. Eli Whitney. The cotton gin was one of the key inventions of the Industrial Revolution.

30. Mercerisation. Almost all the thread that is used in

stitching now is mercerised thread.

31. John Boyd Dunlop.
32. Sulphur is added to natural rubber during vulcanisation.
33. Christopher Sholes, who patented a typewriter in 1868, started collaborating with Remington in 1873 to build and sell his invention.
34. Lewis Waterman who then commercialised his technology and founded the Waterman Company. Waterman pens were sold until very recently.
35. Tinfoil.
36. The triode was invented by Lee de Forest in 1906. He did this by adding another electrode, in the form of a mesh, to the diode which had been invented by Fleming a couple of years earlier.
37. Joseph Lister who used carbolic acid or phenol in his surgery to disinfect wounds. However, because of the irritation caused to the skin by this strong chemical, its use on wounds was discontinued.
38. The first x-ray image taken by Roentgen was that of his wife's hand!
39. Bakelite, which till recently was used in all electrical switches.
40. Chromium.
41. *Penicillium notatum* was the fungus which grew in the equipment of Alexander Fleming when it was accidentally left open. Fleming realised that the fungus gave out some chemicals which killed the bacteria which were being grown in the equipment and hence penicillin was discovered.

42. A catalytic converter has very tiny particles of platinum and palladium which act as catalysts. Unburned petrol and carbon monoxide in the presence of these catalysts, reacts with oxygen from the atmosphere and forms water and carbon dioxide.

43. Seeing in the dark with the help of night vision glasses is possible since they detect infra red radiation and not visible radiation. Ordinary vision is possible because objects which we see reflect the light which falls on them. Infra red radiation is emitted by objects and living things. The night vision glasses detect these and can hence see even though there is no visible light.

44. It is true that aluminium is a good conductor of heat but it is not a good absorber or emitter of radiation. Hence when we wrap food with aluminium foil, the food cannot lose heat by radiation to the surroundings and this keeps it hot.

45. The compact disc player has a tiny laser which produces near infra red radiation which reads the information. The wavelength of the radiation is 780 nanometres (a billionth of a metre) while the wavelength of visible light is between 390-750 nanometres.

46. The current. Although all of the batteries deliver the same voltage, the amount of maximum current is different, with the bigger sized batteries (of the kind needed for torches) delivering higher current. The bigger-sized batteries also contain more stored energy.

47. The metallic mesh on the inside of the door is the sixth side of the cube which is the oven. The purpose of the sides of the cube (oven) is to reflect and hence trap the microwaves inside the enclosure so that the food inside

can be cooked or warmed. A metallic enclosure traps the radiation inside. The wavelength of the microwaves being much larger (around 10 cm), the mesh (which has openings of about a millimetre) doesn't effect the reflection of the microwaves.

48. Cotton basically consists of cellulose which is a kind of sugar. The sugar molecules are linked in long chains in cellulose but these get softened by water. When one irons cotton pants with a little water, the steam produced dissolves into the cellulose chains, softens them and so makes them easier to iron the creases.

49. AM radio signals are relatively lower frequency than FM waves. In the atmosphere there is a layer of conducting material which can reflect off AM waves but not the high frequency FM waves. Hence even though one may not be in the line of the sight of the transmitter, one can still receive AM waves but not FM waves. A similar effect is responsible for our being able to hear short wave radio over long distances (BBC for instance).

50. The TV remote emits infrared radiation which is produced by a LED. The radiation is produced at two different frequencies which allow the signal to be coded in bits—for instance, the high frequency radiation could be used to denote a1 while the low frequency one, a0. When we press different buttons on the remote, different combinations of 1s and 0s are generated which are detected by a small photocell on the TV and interpreted by a microchip inside the TV to perform the desired function.

51. Daniel Fahrenheit who also devised the Fahrenheit scale of temperature.

52. The corn kernel in popcorn contains some starch which is moist. When the kernel is heated to a temperature above the boiling point of water, the water inside turns to steam and as the temperature rises, the steam pressure increases till a point comes when the starch is forced out of the kernel with a popping sound.

53. The silencer or muffler in a car basically slows down the exhaust gases which are coming out from the engine. The exhaust gases which come from the engine are at high pressure and when they are released into the atmosphere, they would produce a popping sound like a firecracker. The muffler or silencer basically reduces the pressure of the exhaust gases and hence reduces the sound produced by them.

54. Global System for Mobile communication and Code Division Multiple Access. These are fundamentally different methods by which mobile communication is possible. In our own country, both of them exist together.

55. The first recorded hybrid vehicle was made by the celebrated automobile designer, Ferdinand Porsche (who later also designed the Volkswagen Beetle), in 1901. This was a petroleum-electric hybrid though, and because of the lack of reliable gears, etc. it never really caught on.

56. Regenerative braking is a system where the electric motors in the hybrid vehicle acts as a generator during braking and this supplies electrical energy to the batteries, thereby charging them up and increasing the range of the vehicle.

57. Instant noodles which he called Chikin Ramen.

58. Jagdish Chandra Bose who also made fundamental inventions in radio technology.

59. Corn flakes, which were first made by Dr. John Harvey Kellogg.

60. Superconducting QUantum Interference Device. These are devices which can measure extremely weak magnetic fields by exploiting quantum interference.